# Edgar
## the Lonely Electron

ISBN 978-1-956010-16-9 (paperback)
ISBN 978-1-956010-17-6 (digital)

Copyright © 2021 by Benedict Maresca

All rights reserved. No part of this publication may be reproduced, distributed, or transmitted in any form or by any means, including photocopying, recording, or other electronic or mechanical methods without the prior written permission of the publisher. For permission requests, solicit the publisher via the address below.

Rushmore Press LLC
1 800 460 9188
www.rushmorepress.com

Printed in the United States of America

I am Edgar the Electron. I live in the Hydrogen atom, which is the smallest element. It is so small that it only has one electron, which is why I am very lonely. Atoms are some of the smallest building blocks in the universe, and are part of everything that has mass. Mass measures the amount of matter in a substance or an object. Matter is all the stuff that exists in the universe.

Every day, I circle around the nucleus of the atom. The nucleus consists of protons and neutrons.

The atom is so small that a grain of sand would seem like a giant planet next to it.

I am so fast that it is impossible to locate me at any time. In fact, everyone is so uncertain about the location of electrons that they call it the uncertainty principle.

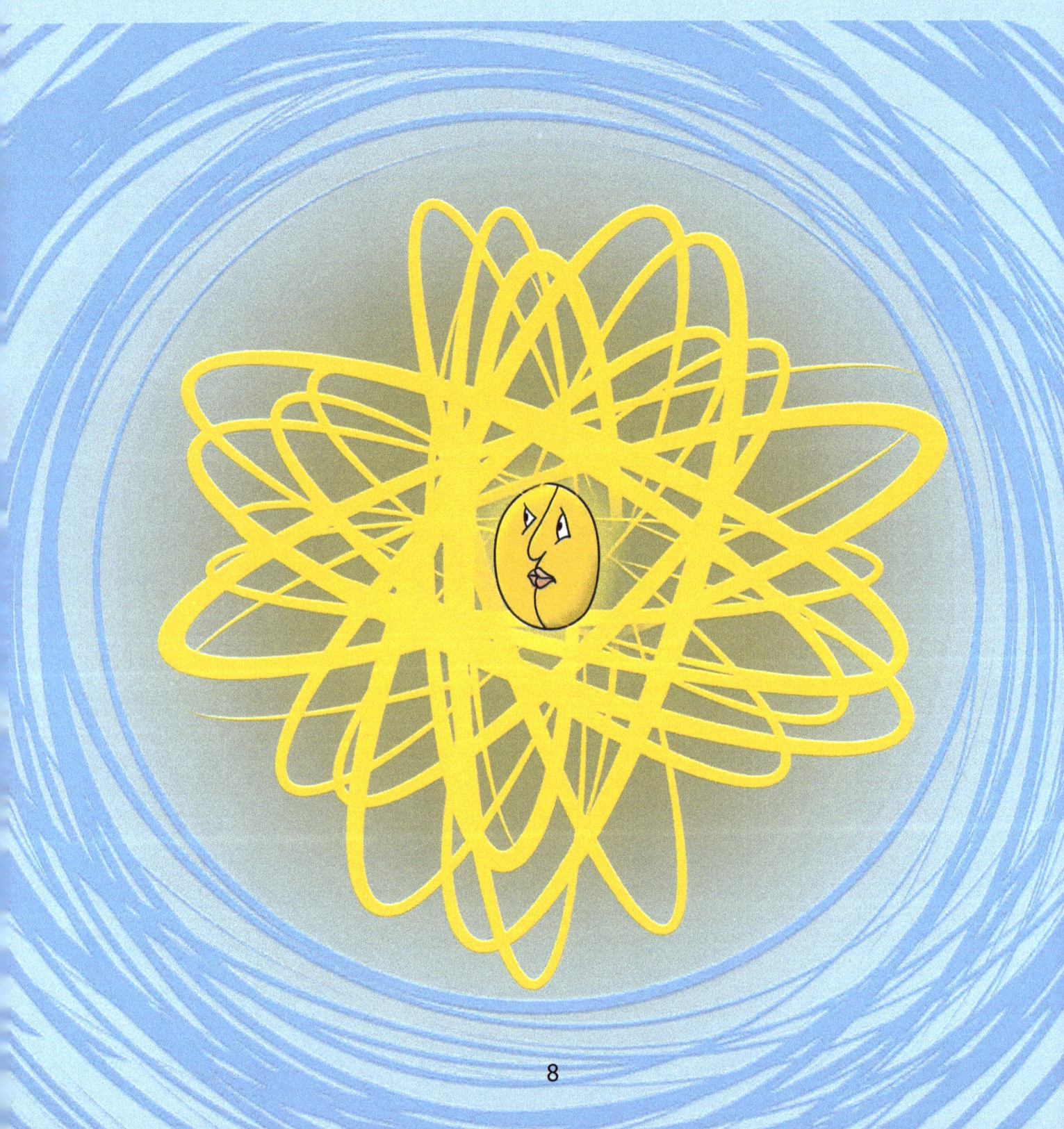

I, as well as my cousins in other atoms, have many jobs. One fun job is running from switches to lights to supply electricity to light bulbs and electrical appliances. Electrons are electricity.

Another job that we do when we are catching some rays is supplying electricity from solar panels. The material on solar panels is made up of atoms of large mass. My cousins that live there can get bumped off when sunlight hits it. This jumping off creates electricity.

I get mad sometimes because I do all the work while my nucleus friends just sit there. It is hard work.

I carry an electrical charge, which is negative. The proton in the nucleus is a positive charge, and the neutron is neutral. The nucleus guys always say I need a better attitude because I am negative.

One fun job we, electrons, do is to be shot out of an electron gun to create a picture on TV screens. I meet a lot of movie stars that way.

Electrons act really different than any other things in the universe. Some people say we have dual personalities—part wave and part particle. I guess that is why I like to surf.

One job that my cousins and I do not like doing is when radioactive compounds like Uranium decompose; they emit electrons, which is called radioactivity. It sure gets hot in there.

So next time you turn on the lights or some music, or pass a solar panel or a nuclear power plant, remember all the hard work that we—electrons—do, and say, "thanks, Edgar."